Forever

Forever the last time

Jim Slominski

Wolsak and Wynn • Toronto

Typeset in Goudy Old Style, printed in Canada by The Coach House Printing Company, Toronto.

Cover design: Coach House
Cover art: Janice Jackson ©2003
Author's photograph: Stephen Dominick ©2004

Thanks to the editors of the following journals and periodicals, in which the poems in this book previously appeared: *Journal of the Writing Space*, *En Route*, and *Niagara Currents*.

The publisher gratefully acknowledges the support of the Canada Council for the Arts and the Ontario Arts Council.

The Canada Council for the Arts | Le Conseil des Arts du Canada

ONTARIO ARTS COUNCIL
CONSEIL DES ARTS DE L'ONTARIO

Wolsak and Wynn Publishers Ltd.
192 Spadina Avenue, Suite 315
Toronto, ON
Canada M5T 2C2

National Library of Canada Cataloguing in Publication Data

Slominski, Jim, 1961-
Forever the last time / Jim Slominski
Poems.
ISBN 0-919897-92-4

I. Terminally ill children—Poetry. 2. Terminally ill children—Family relationships—Poetry. I. Title.

PS8587.L65F67 2004 C811'.6 C2004-900446-8

This book is for Mary, Jake, and Maya

Many thanks to Chris Pannell, Donna Langevin, Mary Ellen Csamer, Kate Weichelt, and Mary Slominski for their insights in helping to shape the poems in this book. Their thoughtful reading and valuable comments on my work are always welcome and appreciated. To Al Moritz, John B. Lee, Laura Lush, and Allan Briesmaster for their kind words and suggestions. Thanks to the Niagara-based writer's group, *Write Off the Deep End*, who have encouraged me and helped me improve many of these poems over the years.

Special thanks to Maria Jacobs for her experience, her skillful eye and ear, her dedication to the craft of poetry, and her quiet support of my work. To Noelle Allen who filled in all the missing spaces.

I'm also very grateful to Janice Jackson for providing yet another beautiful cover to match the music within.

Contents

Eleven

Nowhere in our imaginations did we picture him
still moving about, trot-running with his friends
through the house, zapping each other with lasers?
nowhere did we imagine him this night
still climbing the stairs, straddling them,
leaning on the walls, all the way up, all on his own.
I follow him up and then lie beside him to read him to sleep.
Before he slips away for the night
I whisper to him, *You're amazing.*
And as though he's been waiting
all these eleven years to hear this he sinks into the bed,
into a sleep as soft as waves,
and floats. My hand stays on his back
to hold him there, and keep this birthday
from ever escaping.

Poem soup

First you need a book,
that's your pot.
Then a page, your water.
Chop up some fresh words
straight from the garden. Just right?
not too green, hard and flavourless.
Or overripe, with seed squish
all over the counter:
overused metaphors and landscapes,
roving hills and the grass is green.

Throw the mix into the blender.
Add spice, the ground up
bits of your heart.
Heat the pot, sauté the mix
until golden brown,
hold the boil.
Watch the words bob and roil?
systolic   vortice   perambulate.
Watch them percolate.

Then pour into a bowl.
Something for the eyes, the nose,
a hot soup that waits on the table.
These are poems. Served up
for those just come in
from the snow,
having skied a vast wilderness.

Snow is a muffler

that wraps down
to the boots of the farm.
The snow dust falls like burst sunlight
through a basement window.
Peach trees, laid out
in graveyard rows,
peaceful, accept the falling shroud.

Out there
a flock of sparrows
moves like a tattered flag
loose in the wind, through
distant spruce trees,
silent as tumbleweed.

The stitch of these skis
shears the snow dunes.
It's the only sound.
As well as breath
not catching up to lungs. And
gulped drinks of cold air.

When I pull up to the house, pass
the wheelbarrow by the gate

there's a sudden *scree scree.*
Open-fingered startled flaps.
Flash of colour: the pomegranate of a robin's breast

Instead it's a rusty
red-tail hawk
that escapes upwards
into the bruised clouds
parcelled by telephone wire,

leaving behind a nest
of sparrow feathers – each one its own
tiny bird
taking off across the drifts.

Skating rink

I have to fill the swimming pool today,
I say the same mistake three times
on this cold day, high of minus twelve.
I mean *rink.*
The last-clinging leaf
always dies at the bottom
of this clear miniature lake.
Fence reflections ripple
in a distorted wave,
slowly freezing
into picket soldiers.

Not big enough to really be called a rink.
Three strides across
and over
and out.
Something to capture a wafer of winter on.
Something to scratch our signatures on.

The snow gathers.
I shovel in the moonlight.
Some nights, too cold to skate
it becomes a magnet to draw in the stars.
And here we throw a puck at it
and fake a game on boots
for five minutes
before we're frigid and bored
and a fight breaks loose
over who's in net
and who's on dad's team
and can't we just pass the puck around and
I score! I win!

Then there are nights where the snow
comes down
through the halogen lamp clamped to a maple branch
like snow in a snow-shaker Christmas scene,
and we family-pose a postcard skate,
an instant
of imaginary purity
just outside
of our ability to hold on to it.

Early life

In a muscleless state
you were the fastest fish,
cleverest, swimming there first,
outdoing the others,
finding your way
into the egg.

Then the beautiful way that Mary carried you,
carrying you since she was a little girl,
waiting for you, the round globe
of the world inside her, the blueprint
of life illuminated like stars
on the dark walls. You didn't kick.
Which scared her. Hands rubbed
over the surface
like a fortune-teller on a crystal ball.

Eighteen hours of labour.
Breathing techniques
flew out the window, speared
in the January sun,
became crystals of snow
on rooftops. Pain grew like a tree.

The window between two universes
stayed closed. And, after eighteen hours,
dilation unchanged, they called the doctor.
In another time you would have joined
the long, sad history of others,
of death at birth. Stuck,
couldn't push, already
without strength,
the cord coiled around you.
Life, and one
of its many nooses.

Development

On a stripped orchard the conveyor belts
lift themselves upwards, frozen,
like giant teeter totters
abandoned in the snow
Clumps of hard soil stuck in the rollers.
The belts hover
above sand piles.
The sign says Clean Fill.
For those in need.

I believe the soft peach trees that came from here
will burn fast,
full of sweet sap,
in fireplaces. Another sign: Cheap Wood Available.
What trees did the peaches replace
seventy-five years ago? Hawthorn and hickory,
sugar maple, oak?

A billboard announces
the quartering of land,
a survey:
houses will grow on this spot,
skateboards will flourish, forest green
Jeep Cherokees will slumber in garages,
trees will be captured on the lawns.

The brush lot on the far horizon
sticks up like a crew cut.

One of the last original houses.

The art of the Japanese sword

Open with a kneeling bow.

Adjust your sword
with a sleight of hand,
a calm
as slow as a mountain
shift.

Give
yourself up
to the whole scene, so that
nothing's left

when the blade pulls itself up
out
in a
simple single
stroke. And cut

your opponent's
temple, to release
all the birds that chatter
in his caged head,

and up over
down
to slice into two halves
what was never whole
anyway,
and leave something for the gods
to sew back together.

Fling
the drops of blood
off the blade so that they are
caught, rounded
by air, and then land the way
a Jackson Pollock paint stroke
splatters the canvas,
seeping towards
a still-life
of body and snow.

Observe
how his face becomes a child's
once again,

snowflakes on his eyelash.

Lasagna Queen

Soap suds to the elbow,
she chatters a bird language flow
of *How was your day?*
Bubbles a jingle
stolen from the kids show
playing in the other room.

Counter top cannot take another
empty Mason jar streaked with canned tomatoes,
curled paper of garlic skin,
bottle of olive oil,
bag of spice, hunk of cheese,
spoon, knife, pot,
cup of coffee going cold.

The stove is the sun of the house.
We tan ourselves on aroma.

I hover and await
the breaking of bread
into huge chunks,
to be traffic cop
to meat, noodle, sauce,
point them to the onramp of the fork.
Sop up what's left, and exclaim
Look Mary,
you don't have to wash this dish.

I await the wine,
a half-glass of red,
an autumn ether
that unleashes the colour
of changing leaves inside me.

Across the table I catch her eye
and ask forgiveness,
as at each meal
we utterly devour
her every masterpiece.

Strep Throat

All that's left is the ragged end
of Saturday afternoon, the trees on the horizon
tear holes into the sun
so that it leaks pink light into the clouds.

Perhaps that's the reason Jake starts
to swell with tears at just this moment,
the way a little mouse gnaws
into the hollow of his heart.

Is Maya going to feel better by tomorrow?
She's been asleep all day,
groggy from fever and flu,
hardly with us at all, just a rag of herself.

And Jake has false-started at play all day long,
talking to himself, scripting for his action figures,
laying them in rows on the chess board,
on the dining room table, on the bookshelves.

And then walked away from them, abandoning them
for the TV, the sofa, the bed, the floor.
Restless in his halfness. *Will she be able to play tomorrow?*
He's already feeling Sunday approach,

the way it chops the seconds into guillotine slices
and, far too soon, Monday morning starts to poke through.
Maya answers for me, and croaks, *Don't worry Jake,*
from the other room. Soon she's going to play all the voices

of those waiting toys,
tape the torn clouds back together.

THE CAVE FLOATERS

Let's go Jake
into the buried caves
of Cro-Magnon. Too tricky
for you to be able
to crawl
through the long low tunnels or walk
the craggy slippery paths,
your muscles too weak,
too unsure
of even the smooth ground.

But let's imagine
we can float instead like Chagall creatures,
self-illuminated, and see
outpourings of paintings:
bison mammoth rhino bear.
Reindeer, elaborately-antlered,
that glisten brilliant, and race
the fields of rocky wall.

Hold my hand and we'll go deeper,
squeeze through a narrow hole, close your eyes,
and we'll float
to the opening of the wide cavern beneath.
Where a magnificent sculpture
of a male and female bison,
each two feet long, in the dark,
has been worn by the touch
of ancient humans.

See the child's footprints
that played on a mud ledge forty thousand years ago,
the negative imprint
of the child's hand on the wall.
The father blew ochre pigment onto it,
onto the blackness of stone.
It stayed there all these years.
That was me. That
was your hand.

The first signs

Forsythias pendulous
with gold bloom,
and air that bites the nose
with the smell
of manure being spread.
Spring is here.

Wide fields, in chunks, are turned over
and the small patches beside houses
are ready for onions and early lettuce.
Clothes dry stiff in the wind,
on clotheslines
soon to be extinct.

From a distance, there's the human insect
whirr of sprayers
putting on first applications
of dormant oil, in endless battles
against the six-spotted spider mite.

Farmers in yellow rain suits
covered with oily slick,
sun burnt and bristled faces,
come home for coffee,
and a little shot.

On their minds:
before long, wave after wave of candied perfume.
Before long, cherry blossoms
and endless chores. Faint yearnings
for the despised
and departed snow.

Tai Chi before birds awake

The slow push and pull
of Tai Chi that goes nowhere
in particular, circles, burns itself
out to the morning like a flame
on a matchstick.
I caress
the darkness of the living room

and breathe in and out
Thoughts grow
out to the sofa,
mingle in the corners
with dust,

become those endless stories and conversations
with the world
that I carry
and, inwardly, silently,
rehearse.

Only every now and then,
are they flipped
out of my hands
by small, exact movements
as though they are opponents
thrown flat on their backs.
I too am stunned
by how rare
and fragile these moments.

Nightshade

Nightshade, our perfectly black cat.
Even his nose is black, Maya is fond of saying.
named by Jake the moment he saw him.
Purrs on my lap, my arm, my book as I try to write.
Rubs so that my pen makes trails in the letters,
choppy stones form words.
The bowl must be empty.

We try to keep this one indoors,
having lost all the previous ones
to the coyotes wandering the fields out back.
The ones that didn't come home
from their night excursions,
and days later I would find
their mangled bodies
looking like dirty mops,
purrs and meows silenced
into a permanent yawn
in the mud.

He rubs me again,
shaking these words across the page,
and then goes to lean his forepaws
onto the screen door. Stands and cranes.
I hear birds. I imagine those wild dusty cats,
born out of the barns, sending signals.
His blackness is the velvet of night without stars.
He yearns to slip into the vast ocean of darkness
and blend.
His bad luck is just beginning.

Under covers

Cold spring fog hugs
the stark lamplight.
Slips down
branch tip, into house
through pores of mortar, and cracks
in windows and doors,
through blanket,
through skin
to the channel
of marrow in my bones.

The heater's on but does nothing;
heats only the bookshelves
and a stool. Deeper into the blanket I go
until I reach Jake's body,
his soft dough of warmth. Up against him
I steal as much as I can
while he sleeps, gather and build
a hot glow that turns away
the damp air in folds.
We radiate a while.

Slowly I have to get up,
to start my day. And once started
there's no turning back,
no getting back to this one moment.
My body pulls away
from him with the sadness
of a tearing page.

Haiku I

Sound of fierce
night winds
leaving

unveils,

beneath, a field
of spring crickets

At a Canada Day celebration

I see the other boys,
heads shaved down
to the fuzz of a sumac whip,
bodies carved out of sturdy oak,
a summer bronze.
They kick the ball, climb ladders,
hang off trees, whoop and holler.
The air is theirs.
At nine years already working at
being better than their fathers,
slicing the way with the sharp bone
of their chests.

My boy's body
moves like a marionette
made of bricks. No one listens
as ears move too fast
and away. His words
fall against the plexiglas around him.
Wherever he goes, they've all been
five minutes earlier. Still
the sadness, which peels away layers
like an acid inside me,
hasn't caught up to him yet.
It's a shadow that follows
not yet joined to the soles of his feet.
He's in the oblivious love
of his friends,
catching life
from the swirls of air
as they pass.

The southern shores of Lake Ontario

Against a sand and pebble lip
the *lap slap lap slap*
is the thin pulse of a massive creature
whose heartbeat is so deep
it cannot be heard by human ears.
Waves pat the shoreline
cautiously, gently
as though trying to tame land.

Three sparrows
slice the edge of where sky meets lake,
an inch above water
like skimmed stones,
catching blends of purple-blue shattered
light reflections
off a pastel salmon sunset.

All the while a kingfisher flits
back and forth,
from the grey dry torso
of the rooted driftwood
snapped maple back
to a live one, its leaves covered in tar spot.

Stops
mid air. Hovers
hummingbird fashion, beak sharpened
to a mosquito point. Poises.
Drops
dead stone splash,
three seconds under.

And emerges with a minnow,
in rapid flight,
a getaway
to the safe shores.
Like it just stole something
from under
the sleeping giant's pillow.

Lineage

I see my father, in a snippet of memory,
working in his front patch of garden
laying stones in the hot sun.
He bolts upright in a sudden backward slide
like a fast-moving crab and then,
recovered, moves forward again
with a shovel and swings down,
and squashes the spider.

As his father probably did.
And I too, watching and learning?
learning to look for spiders in every dark corner,
between the blades of long grass
where they tunnelled webs?
watch especially for them
strung between the cedar hedges,
orbed, waiting face height,
the strong sticky snip sound of web line snapping,
noticed too late,
a ten-year-old screeching for his mother.

I'd watch their every move
to be sure I knew where they were,
what they were doing.
Not of the insect world, more like animal,
detached hands on legs of fingers.
And conscious.

Later, as an adult, I took photos
of the slow moving Argiope and his mate,
that crawled over the broken boards
of the old barn we tore down,
fascinated by their size,
the elephant of the northern spider world,

their black and yellow striped bodies
like exotic candy.
Drawn to that electric surge.

And now on those quiet summer afternoons,
pulling weeds or trying to read a book,
and, while the kids are playing,
there's a squeal,
a shriek of *Daddeee!* I know
the long thread of lineage
remains unsnipped.

Mary's morning

She wakes up, and dreams
slip away through finger nets
like strands of seaweed floating
out   out
on the tide

She turns to the weight
of the clock
which metronomes
its schedules, and her heartbeat bends

like the first fresh growth
of ivy,
burdened by a load
of heavy frost.

Down to the kitchen
Is there any fresh coffee?
Relaxes a little
into a chair, at the table
something to read, music on,
for just a moment
just one   minute   more   always
on the edge of leaping
springing into

Got to make the kids' lunch
Where's my work apron
Have to defrost the bread
Get the kids' clothes from the dryer
Put their socks on
Am I forgetting something

Fill in school forms get knapsacks put books in
Onto school bus
Brush my hair
Off to
work

never ends. And
out of this emerges,
as from the long lean shoots
of twenty-year bamboo,
her rare flower,
slow to open
but deep the roots.

Reading lesson

Jake reads to me at four o'clock
in the morning. I coax him into Dr. Seuss,
after our sleepy talk, under a feather blanket,
about his fear
of books
and us, his fear
of our disappointment in him.
My head swims in an ocean
of air
that I can't breathe.
Not so Jake. Never.

So I find a book on the shelf,
gather him, and he reads
sitting on my lap with the soft *shush*
of early morning rain.
I can remember already reading
thick books at his age.
And now I write my own,
I tell myself, to blaze a path for him.

But he sees me instead
as a giant
who can crush him, leaving him
in the swirl of my abilities,
in a swim of disembodied letters
broken
like loose formations of geese
following each other
off the sky of the page.

MIDNIGHT SNACK

Ants on the kitchen counter
Stop/Start   rotate-search,
antennae-feel
like aimless
remote control cars
guided by a three-year-old.

Two bump blindly
oh excuse me and move on.

Beside some empty Mason jars
ten have discovered an oasis
of invisible sticky spill,
and form a meditation ring
of stillness
on the spot, humming
a harvest mantra.

Another discovery,
ant-miles away,
near the old peanut butter jar
filled with almonds and walnuts:
two milk cookies left at the bottom
of a torn-away cellophane wrapping.
Something major here, calling for reinforcements,
enough to sustain civilisation
for another million years.
Cargoes of crumb are carted
by drunken pirates
to the corner behind the cutting board.

Others stay behind
to extract their fill of the booty,
sucking on a cookie, motionless.
As I would have done:
just let it melt into softness
in my mouth.

Meditation Practice

We start the day in overwhelming silence.
except of course that the electricity hums,
and the wind quakes the birch outside,
and the cat meows for attention:
food, a spot on the lap, a lust
for outside.

And then there's our breathing.
Always out of sequence, out of sync
like clocks set at different paces,
merging and drifting apart.
And there's the ornate noisiness
of our separate hearts, and the wild ride
on the dragon's scaly tail
of our thoughts, as we remind ourselves,
It's only thinking, only thinking.

Then, as always, the dragon puts his foot through our boat
which creates one helluva leak.
In come thoughts, the water, and out comes
the bailing bucket again.
In comes more. And out.
And the knots in the wood start chanting a perfect *Om* –
the grains and whorls of the wood, the O's they form,
the dark wetness like mysterious, textured words
from the deep bottom of the past,
from a long lineage of masters.

Except that
the boat is now completely immersed,
sinking, just as
the dragon's tail flicks out of sight.

Right where we started.
Where we always were,
birch boughs shaking,
cat at the window.

Night storm

Relentless winds rock the house,
chestnut branches scratch fiercely to get in.
Everything's caught in a horizontal force,
I imagine cows flashing past.
And then the power goes out,
the sudden silence of which wakes Jake and Maya.
Loud *brkkahs* of thunder in the pitch dark
send them shrieking for us
along the hollow halls.
We all go downstairs,
and huddle on the sofa and floor,
Mary and I each with a child.
We fall asleep
with the persistent lightning outside,
and the light of one low candle.

In the morning we hear
that the lakeshore in the Old Town
has been clawed by a tornado.
Hundred year old trees ripped up and spilled
across town roads, and onto farms.
Lampposts down, transformers,
sidewalks pulled up and cracked
like wafer biscuits,
oak roots plucked out
like turnips.

We only see the cleanup afterwards,
creeping the town in our car,
traffic-jammed with other curiosity-seekers:
limbs in tidy heaps, trunks sectioned
like diced carrots,
that could become outdoor furniture now
under the cleansed sapphire skies of a summer barbecue.

We get out to walk, and where a spruce fell
Jake finds a fresh cone in the root hole,
picks it up, keeps it, thinking
that it was preserved beneath
the tree the whole time.
And I go along with it,
not wanting to discourage
his metaphor
of a new beginning.

Fugue in dark green

It's a high day
with shape-naming clouds:
train   crocodile   dog-chasing-squirrel.
And beneath feet, moss on rocks.
And beneath rocks, river
moving fast
as though pouring from a bottle.
And child

with parents. It's a high day of
green shadow   thick bush   forest
sliced with shards
of sunlight. Along the ledge
a child with twig in the water.
Parents watch

the high wheel of seagulls,
intricate as watch gears
dip   rest   fish
one replaces
the other over
and over above the high green river.
A small twig slips

into the day beneath the river
and hand reaches low
stretches   reaches   hand
a tiny arm
into the green sky
while clouds flash past
fast forward.

High days forever slipping. Reaches
too far.   In.   Slips
too fast. Too tiny
an arm to reach up, to stretch up to green
sky of bush and sunlight flash,
to reach parents. Arms stretch
and flash past,
forever
the last time.

Schoolyard

Jake beats on Maya because
she's reading with mom. It bugs him
that he can't. Calls her names,
yells at her, comes raging into the room
threatening that he's going to kill her,
stab her with a knife.
This is all very familiar.

Ok Jake, what happened at school today? Nothing.
What happened? I don't want to go to school.
I want to get sick and die!
Typical Jake responses
to a deep sadness buried
in the honeycomb of his heart.
And we brace ourselves, living in the shadow
of falcons, waiting for them
to swoop in
and slice away pieces.

What happened? He tells us
about coming in late from recess,
all the other kids
already working on their schoolwork.
About being at the far end
of the field, of the playground,
searching for insects with his friends,
excited that they had found
a praying mantis the day before.

Then the bell rings and everyone runs
and he can't keep up
and his friends get smaller
and no one waits
and he tries

to run fast
falling further
and further behind.
Alone. Crying.
A rag doll
tumbles through his chest, an awareness
crushes him
like the body of a praying mantis
under a friend's shoe.

Roadside crow

This crow is a symbol
of our love for symbols,
sitting on top of this autumn birch
like a puncture in the sky.
Clings to the last greenness
that slips into orangeyellowred
yet one more time.

I see all crows in this one–
all those bodyguards
of picnic tables and grape posts
weighing down this slender twig.

The even wing
thrusts against the edge of the winter wind
and takes all these crows
in one body

to the next dying elm,
another telephone pole,

a cornfield, the next cornfield
and the next,
searching for grubs
pecking among the sweet eyes
blindfolded in husks.

What's down there

Silhouettes of dry grass bend
against the basement window
exotic, elegant as
bamboo in a Japanese print.

Then there's this mess.
Boxes, clothes, old toys.
Do the laundry,
and run.

Like I used to when I was a boy,
when I'd imagine a genie hand
with eight green snake arms
growing, slithering out
to catch me from behind a scratched bureau
or a pile of mattresses.
The click of the furnace
was a gun being cocked
by hidden assassins, those big kids
from up the road
that chased me home one day.
Streak up the stairs, my body pounding,
and lock the door behind me.

And down here now, how much safer is it?
The assassins have grown old.
They are the fine hair
of cobwebs on rafters,
are the black mould on walls.
Incessant rain has filled and flooded,
ruined wood pallets, old clothes.

Destroyed
a baby high chair
that we'd saved purely for the sake of memory.
We had to throw it out.
Almost crying, almost remembering
our children (and ourselves,
almost seeing ourselves) sitting there
in majestic baby bodies, picking at the peas
one by one
with tiny dimpled fingers
as if they were chopsticks.

A long hard day

Arms paddle the air for balance
as though he's swimming.

Tries his best, his very hardest,
moves his absolute fastest.
Still we have to wait for him.

Straddles the stairs to climb,
leans full weight on the handrail,
two hands to pull up to each step.
I follow ready to catch his fall.

Can't sit still. Squirms, fidgets.
Muscles too weak to hold his body like an arrow.

Knocks stuff off tables, drops books, spills drinks,
as he moves in big chunks around the room.

And falls into our arms when day is done.
So much work to stay alive.

Releases himself to sleep, his favourite time.
When gravity asks nothing more of him.

Picking out burrs

He remembers small things, little snips,
from when he was young.
Remembers being on a train ride, the fields are green and gold
in the long light of sunset. He's with his mother.
He's wearing his blue sweater, his favourite,
the one with the big blue buttons
and two white bands on the right sleeve.
His brother has the same one, only red.
They pass cows that are orange sunset-dipped statues
staring vacant, except it seems like
they're looking at him.

He remembers something about his grandfather,
in a room. Someone else's living room, not theirs.
But it's their furniture,
same burst flowing leaf pattern, deep crimson,
same dustiness, same doilies on the armrests.
But not their room. It's raining big drops
against the window. Everything is dark and grey.
It's just him and his grandfather,
the smell of must coming from the sofa.
Not a word.

And something else. His mother takes him
through a field. Just for a walk, she says.
He's wearing his favourite sweater. They gather burrs.
He wants to take them off, picks at them,
but little pieces stay stuck in
like the claws of tiny creatures that won't let go.
The sun is setting, the shadow
cuts a deep blue from the buildings.

The air is cold. She takes him through
a maze of streets. They find a red car.
Their car. Parked on a street
in front of an apartment building.
His father's car. His mother says nothing,
does nothing, just holds his hand tighter,
colder, tries to hide that she's crying,
and walks back the way they came,
through the streets, the field.
And all along the way he keeps
picking at the burrs.

Haiku II

Sudden shower
of gold
leaves

grasps helplessly

at the sunset

Six is my favourite number

At any first meeting Maya tells everyone
about our new kitten
but we don't know
if it's a boy or a girl,
and our new sofa
that's also a bed.
Opens our house to them with tours.
Six is my favourite number
because I'm six years old now.
Our hostess. Our dramatist,
who takes things to extremes
of the play, exiting with
No one loves me!
indignation mixed with Southern charm,
the belle of the kitchen ball, a magnolia
wrapped in honeysuckle crepe.

She recites a poem
that she learnt in school last year,
remembers it and performs it
because, as she reminds us, it's
almost autumn.
A poem about coloured leaves
and falling, and she falls with them.

And I fall too
for this princess of plush puppies,
an old king
who looks on and claps
as she plays
in the courtyard,
by the rose vines, where
walkways wind and doorways loom.

She offers a drawing of crayon wildflowers,
a bouquet of purples,
I picked them myself.
Do you like them?
But disappears
down the long stone corridor
before I can answer.

Mr Stripes

Mr Stripes ate a poisoned mouse
from the poisoned neighbour-field
of crop rotating corn.
Sat all afternoon on a stump
by the brush fire, staring
at a tree ring or a grain.
I thought he was trying to get warm
or was a Buddha cat
who gathered his powers
by just sitting.

When it was time to go
we pushed him to wake up,
and he fell over and wobbled, walking.
We carried him to the barn.

At night I brought him up to my bed.
Warm. Wouldn't move.
Breathed
from his throat, barely,
and woke me twice, chilly,
with thin meowling cries
in the silent rooms upstairs.
The second time, I felt his breath
stop, his tiny
heart pulse stop.
And nothing.
Then stretched with a long purr
and was stiff.

I buried him by the barn
breaking the hard crust of cold soil,
into the soft belly under.
And then soaped and rinsed my coat,
that he had lain on
with open pupils all night,
to take out the strange
oily stain of death.

Late autumn heat wave

I can't help but think of giant holes in the ozone,
like those cartoon cannon balls
that tear though the soft tissue of cloud.
Or bare patches of grey
all over the surface of the earth
like a sick man with his hair falling out in clumps,
where the trees have been chopped
to make way for dust farms.

That's what I think about when we're out
mid-November, working in our t-shirts,
the sunset a necklace of crimson and gold.
Where's the sludge, the sleet, the slop,
the rain that pours off our hoods
into our collars, down our boots?
The snow that's a messy brown package
delivered by a miserable and soaked
postman of the skies,
travelling by donkey?
Or those dry days of knife-sharp, cloud-peeling
lapis lazuli sky, a frigid call ahead from January
coming in on the North train?

A little worried I admire
the vermilion glory of this sunset,
and the beauty of the world
caught on fire,
a dangling pendant of flames
twirling through the velvet universe.
The leaves are in the last throes of passion
like salmon making their futile leaps
against a dark certainty.

Are there still fish at the bottom of the ocean?
Or have we cleared that too,
to display a swimming pool sapphire blankness?
All in the image of ourselves.
That perfect mirror reflection
of the vacuity
of the smiling sky
that we've now employed
to handshake for hollow votes.

Haiku III

Winter's arrival:
on a barren road

fine snow
swishes

like a cat's tail

The Christmas Party

When Jake unravels into a tantrum
we can't pretend to know how his body
makes a series of lonely voices
for him to listen to,
like so many starlings
above an abandoned vineyard.

We don't know the vinegar sting
on his open wounds
as Maya, his younger sister, cartwheels in front of him
or flings herself into jumping jacks.
Reads past him. *How come she read those books,*
and I can't?

Or when we're at a Christmas party
with other children with terminal illnesses,
and they announce that
a girl died yesterday, only fourteen.
And the kids with Cerebral Palsy
loll in their wheelchairs,
their eyes sharp
as trapped panthers.

One boy with MD like Jake, but older,
in a chair, can't move,
wears splints, just had an operation,
rods tied to his spine. Takes it all in,
slowly watches:
puppets and painted faces and
fishing for penny prizes and
sand art in plastic bottles.
The line-up to sit on Santa's lap.

We watch Jake slip into that line
and feel
like our skin is being peeled away.

TOYSTOYSTOYS

Just as I'm raging at the kids about the house needs tidying and no one cleans up but me and look at all these toys and we never had this many when we were kids going to stuff them all into a big garbage bag and throw them out with Thursday's trash and other kids help out around the house why can't they and if they don't start picking up after themselves I'm going to bring all these PokemonStarWarsBatmanToyStoryDigimonGodzillaBeanieBabies to the Salvation Army and give them to children who have nothing and who appreciate the things they get

I imagine
years from now
the sounds of laughter and fighting
and dialogue for action figures improvised on the spot
gone

and me
opening boxes
weeping trying desperately
to shake
the life back into them

From the Barn to the House

Dog-howls echo off the moon,
pull in a sky so low and sharp
I can see the stars between the stars,
the *milky* in Milky Way.
Constellations skate over
a crisp, clear blackness that almost snaps,
setting up for morning frost.

They look down on us,
and our million years
are just a millisecond.

Old friends.
Orion draws his bowstring, sword at hip,
poised to launch his arrow over the Pleiades.
Big Dipper dips
down to scoop,
from the cold mountain river,
some pebble-stars and ink.

THE WORST BASS STUDENT

I was, without doubt, the worst student.
The one it didn't come natural to.
The one that started too late.
No stories about having to stand on a stool
when I was nine, sawing on the strings
of Grandpa's Czech double bass.

Mine was a cheap Japanese plywood,
lacquered to a plastic shine,
registering the depth of a transistor radio.
Worked one summer as a hell-hole dishwasher for.
Emitted the sound of a sick bird,
never quite meeting up to the legend
of Charlie Parker blowing everyone away
playing on a plastic sax.

I woke my teacher way too often
from his jazz hangover,
with a series of out-of-tune
slurred intonations, searching desperately
for the sweet centre of the note
like a blind man that finds can openers and spoons
while looking for the corkscrew.
One hour lessons
were cut quickly to half.

Then I'd go home and practice
in my parent's east end basement,
polishing down two pots of perked coffee.

Chase after the metronome beat
like it was a mouse. Simandl Scale Studies open
on the stand, beneath Rufus Reid's Evolving Bassist
with its walking bass notes
spiralling Hickory Dickory
beyond and over the clock,
out of the reach of my hands.

Oh yes, my hands. Each a different brain
feeling for a field-wide connection between left and right,
between notes, melody, rhythm, memory
and the bass,
this huge football fumbled
always at the goal line.

And yet, like a teen in love,
spurned by the girl on the first date,
did not give up, instead went deeper
into that rich growl,
in love with love itself,
ignoring all its rejections.

Cowgirl witch

I'm home with them today. School's been cancelled.
Tree branches groan and creak with weight and wind.
The ice is thick and dangerous on the roads.

She interrupts me in the middle of something
with an on-running conversation that's like two or three birds
chattering on a morning tree.
How much I turn away from what I'm doing, fully or slightly distracted,
half-listening, says something about me, my lack of attentiveness,
my willingness to enter the oblivion of speed
or The Importance of Work, and peddle away my moments to the future–
When I have more time...
But this time I stop.
Dad, can you help put my sleeve over my gloves. She has on her purple wool gloves
with the fake glued-on jewellery beads.
I pull her purple turtleneck sleeves over them.
She wears a skirt, a shiny winter vest, fake leather boots,

and last: an enormous witch's hat.
And here she waits, her arms open wide.
One last detail, one final touch that no cowgirl witch can do without:
a hug. I swoop down and squeeze. And feel
all her small bones inside her growing body, share a glimpse
of her imagination, that complex and beautiful shifting cloud
filled with ice and snow that floats through her.
And off she goes, pistol in one hand, broomstick in the other,
whooping all the way up to the ceiling.

THE ORCHESTRA THAT WOULD BE A TRAIN

Squeal of rust
on ribbons of steel:
violins shriek, *Cardiac arrest!*
Double basses wrestle bassoons
in a stomp of woolly mammoths.
Cellos unravel their sounds
like leather grips
from old golf clubs,
strips tousle
to the floor.

Trumpets bleat out
in imitation
of sheep caught in barbed-wire.

The whole orchestra tips.
The French Horn reels and crashes
into the *Flûte à Bec*
like a drunk
falling
into a drum kit.

The baton jabs helplessly
at some space between the notes
while the conductor's face burns
from being too close to the coal flame. It all ends

on an awkward
lonely honk,
the flightless goose
of an oboe.

Exquisite silence.

Lost boy

Jake plays a Lost Boy
in Peter Pan, in a school play.
Just follows the others
–Jacob, "he who follows"–
walks behind, always last.
Face made up to have dirt on it,
helps shoot down the Wendy-bird,
sits with the "Injuns", captured by pirates,
then fights them with a sword, always
in that lovely lost way of his.
The others look less lost,
sharper, remembering their lines,
their positions, more aware
of the audience, of
who's watching.

Maya sees the play twice, once with us,
once during the day with the school.
She comes home sad. I listen
from the other room
as Mary gently pries open
the lid of melancholy.

A girl in grade two said
that the grade fours were laughing
at Jake because he didn't spin
like the others when the pirates caught them.
We didn't laugh though,
none of the grade ones laughed.

And it's true, he didn't spin,
couldn't, very close to the edge
of the stage, my fear
on the edge with him.
He just walked through
the arms of the pirates
as the rest whirled like tops
from one set of arms to the next.
For effect.

What Maya says hits that same spot
in my chest that seems always
to be reserved for Jake.
Then she finds a deeper spot,
penetrates yet another layer
to a place less touched,
where I try to forget.

The girl said "What was Jake
in a play for anyway? By grade four
wasn't he supposed to be
in a wheelchair?"

As I walk into the room,
Maya's eyes are the saddest
I've ever seen – Maya, who can
play a pout, fake a tear
for a cup of apple juice.
She looks distant,
deep inside of her tiny self, re-assembling
the jumble of lessons
she's beginning to learn.

Observations 3 A.M.

A bout of mild insomnia.
I lie on the sofa on the main floor
and hear the soft movement
of bodies in their beds,
upstairs, in other rooms,
head boards knock against the walls,
sheets and blankets rustle,
tucked in dreams
a mumble of cryptic monologues
pulled out from their basement.

Then at times silent for a long while.
All at once, like an orchestral finale,
everyone suddenly

stirs in unison,
as though something joined in sleep
ignites
a dry grass fire
that runs along a ditch.

And then quiet again.
Except the ticking:
light rain against the windows,
a little wind slap
to punctuate the silence,

the distant clock, only faintly heard,
its lazy tock
like a drippy faucet,

and the mouse
behind the bookshelf
reading my Shakespeare
with his teeth.

Back roads

On my way home, the weather
flexes its muscle,
and pours a heavy rain from the east,
a rare recoil
from the Atlantic
all the way back
onto the Great Lakes.

Trees along the gravel road glisten
in the cloudburst.
They lose a battle with the hydro poles and telephone wires:
the gaping cuts
through their bare April canopies
are like the truncated limbs
of war vets,
stark monuments.

Winds slash through the clothes
that are out to dry by a farmhouse.
They are wet ghosts in the dusk.
Saying something hopeless
beside a warm yellow
square of kitchen light.

Spine

Our spine–a snake design
passed on,
borrowed from the Burgess Shale
worm. Add a heavy head along the road,
rib cage, serpentine dactyl extremities,
hide the tail.

His is not a broken snake,
just a weak one, the load too heavy,
too upright. Something missing for him
from this ancient design,
he climbs
on his tip toes
to compensate for gravity's
relentless pull.
With less and less muscle
to help him, Jake's spine
begins to collapse and curve back:
a fold at mid-point while he stands,
a small furrow I can
slip a finger under,
that I wish I could erase
with invisible hands,
smooth like a tablecloth.

When he was a baby
all the vertebrae fit
into my forearm,
and I rocked him to sleep,
in the thick black night
of the ocean floor.

Drought

Hard-baked topsoil.
Concretised. Can't even scoop
a pailful
for some potted plants
without getting out a jackhammer.

The relentless eyeball of the sun
tries to burn us like paper
with its magnifying glass.

Viburnums, planted just this year,
are going
going gone,
the leaves as crisp
as a crackling fire.

The lawn is a cartoon man
crawling out from the desert,
parched, begging the sun
for a cup of water,
My Kingdom for a . . .

Too late. Bony weeds
have taken over
and cover this graveyard of grass.

The needles I'm pulling
from my bare feet are from the spruce
that's turned dry
and red-eyed,
shedding this old life
for a new kind of death.

The Barber

My grandpa was a barber from the old country,
from a time when they shaved at the barber's every day,
got a haircut every week.
This is what I tell everyone when asked
why I love to trim plants.

Thousands of round heads.
A much easier task than his?
a miscalculated cut doesn't bleed,
no little kids to squirm
as the itchy hairs fall over their face.
Totally at my command.
Spin their pots, a little touch here,
a nip there, catch the low-hanging branches
with secateurs pulled from a holster.

No need to ask the style, square or round at the back?
will that be a trim, crew cut, off the side, flat top,
flip back, fold over the bald spot?
A spirea cut is a spirea cut.
Juniper, juniper.

How my heart wavers at a sound that's much like
the snip-snip in the air
of his old barber's scissors:
the sweet sound of oil and the steel-on-steel whisper
on a new set of hedge trimmers,
singing *shee shee* like a blackbird hidden in a tree.

I boot each pot back into line,
calling for the next,
as my grandpa's life flicks out to the wind
like tiny hairs
every snap of the sheet.

Smallness

Life wants to return us
to smallness. That's why we have bones
that fall apart into something
that can be held in our hand.
And why we have graveyards
that shrink our lives into dates
as though they were baseball statistics.
Reduced to silence out there in the long field.

We can still think greatness is our ultimate quest,
but who was the greatest
ant that ever lived,
which was the greenest blade of grass?
The kitchen window
is a small work of art.
A changing scene every day:
clouds in motion, rain, wind, snow,
the yellow face of sunlight burst onto the walls.
The woodpecker drills at the silver maple
and, after his week with us,
flies off.

Night time pours in through this window.
You wait in bed for me.
A full lifetime
before midnight,
as I fall asleep putting the kids to sleep.
The smallness of us
when I finally slide under the covers beside you
and we both slip beneath the surface
of recorded time.

Gone fishin'

for Mark S.

It's my first time fishing with the kids. I haven't been since I was a youngster myself, the days of going with my dad in the big ponds of the Eastern Townships: Lac Brome, Magog, Lac St. Jean, surrounded by long matted grass, filled with spiders ready to leap at my head. I remember that. I remember The Record for Catching the Most Fish in One Day (in my own mind?cheers rise as I accept the award): eighteen perch (the same one over and over), while no one else caught anything.

I untangle the fishing hook and line beside the van, kids underfoot looking for something to do, their hands in the tackle box, hands on the fishing pole. *Hook hook hook,* fear branching silver under my skin. *Watch out. Someone's going to get hurt.* I check for the first aid kit under the seat. Just in case.
How can I help, Dad?
By not touching anything.

I've got the hook and sinker ready. Jake carries the bobbers, Maya the tackle. I've got the pole, the worms, the knife, the pliers. We walk through the tall sun-parched grass (*Don't mention spiders*) to the calm green lagoon formed off of Twelve Mile Creek. Green scum floats motionless like the first swirl in a gallon can of barn paint.

Where to sit? There are no large rocks, but lots of dog doo. *You can use the tackle.*
Where do I sit then?
Take turns becomes the opening line for a fight of Who-First. I've got a squirmy worm on the hook, bobber on the line. The kids are bored before the first cast. And the first one is lame; my arm too high, trying to avoid a snag on the tall grass. And again it's *hook hook hook*: hook on arm, hook in eye, flash of silver fear.

Stand back! My second cast is better, the third better yet. The kids take turns reeling it in.
Are we going yet?

No, just one more. Another three casts. Then the bobber bobs, *tug tug*. I think, *Ah, here's the fight*. Kind of. I reel it in, and it bobs up, then down again, but no weight, no pole bend.
I think I've got something. C'mon Jake pull it in! Jake? . . .Maya?
Dad, are we going soon?

I drag the line, a slice through scum, to the water's edge. Now it jumps at the surface. It's the sort of jump a large lump of wet weed would make. It's a small white carp, glinting platinum and rainbow off the sun.
Look kids! Look! We got one!
Just looks like one of those fish at the store, the ones on top of ice.

I pull him out easy, like he's already dead. Like he must have been asleep, eating in his sleep, having a dream of being pulled up to surface, out of the pond, into the flat world of the sun, surrounded by three vague shadows.

I put on the gloves, out comes the hook.
Doesn't that hurt the fish, Dad?
They say it doesn't, but I'm not so sure. I toss it back into the water. It makes a dark plonk, the music of *It Never Happened.*

NIGHT SPLINTS

Jake is getting better
is what we tell Mary's mom,
a soft-light lie
for the elderly, for those
battered sea-borne hearts
that cannot take the news
of another squall.

But, in fact, he is doing better,
with steroids to stabilise muscle.
At twelve, he can still bike swim play.
Doing better, as he resists
and fights in a fist rage
with his younger sister,
the one he sees now
as better than him in everything.

Doesn't even need
his night splints
with the velcro straps any more,
he says.
The ones for keeping his ankle flexors
stretched.
They lie by the rocking chair
we bought when he was born,
that I carried upside down on my back
from the furniture store
across the road, wearing it like an outrageous helmet.

They lie by our bed
growing smaller as he ages,
beside each other,
empty moulds
like two hands joined
in plastic prayer.

First love

The early summer mornings,
fresh as long grass

cut down,
that greenness, is what drew me

to ride my bike
around her block miles

and miles away, hoping
she would come out

by accident, and I would
happen to be passing.

My heart skipping and shaking
at each pass, what if

she comes out, what if
that white door opens

and she smiles, and I could be
close enough to see

the light hair
on her arms. I just happened

to be passing, over and over,
round and round the same block,

by accident, on this road.
The air sang a green shade

over me, for just a moment,
before the harsh sun baked the ground

on the empty baseball diamond,
at the park where I would go

when she once again
did not open the door.

Clifford and Jake

Here's how they meet:
Jake bops into the room
doing his best Jake-trot
head-bob arm-weave
to the syncopated notes
of Brownie's trumpet,
matching frenzy and heat
to Max Roach's drum shots.

This big old music
soaks the walls
and Jake dances
toward his bed. Clifford's hard swing,
that spheres beyond the bones
of instruments,
pulls Jake beyond
his muscles, a lightness,
times him to the
beat beat beat
and lands him in bed
with a bounce.

I promise him jazz dreams,
and he knows what I mean
even if I don't. His hand still tapping,
head on pillow, eyes
closed. Smile. A handshake
from Clifford Brown
that breaks through how many
worlds, how many
stories of life-cut-short,
his hand outreached,
notes stopping on
the last punch
as his car crumples forty-five years ago
when he was only twenty-five.

Ritual

She takes the children out of the house
to play in the driveway.
She listens to their voices.
The sun cuts through the bone of winter,
an illusion of spring.

Her hair is ravens' wings in the wind.
She rakes old leaves, snips dry stems.
The kids play. They take their animal friends
out to the rock, beside columbines
buried deep in frozen ground.
The animals have different voices
that they have given them. She rakes beside them,
follows wherever they go, as though
the moon
expresses not only the physics of gravity,
but of loneliness, of
not wanting to float away.

They play with hockey sticks
that were frozen into the ice rink
the day it thawed and froze again,
and trapped them so they became
like fish calling for help.
She can't tell what game they're playing.
The sticks are being used
as staffs, their voices float
in and out of her.

She carries the leaves in the palm of her rake
to the old vegetable garden, spreads them there,
the first place the sun softens
and the heat has a smell
that her body remembers.

Her hair is trapped ravens, flapping wings.
She hears voices in and out,
different voices for each animal.
The sun breaks through the bone.
The moon follows, floats
always in the direction
of voices and light.

How little my good health

Can we say of the sky
that it looks healthy?
Well, tonight it does.
Gold-and-turquoise sunset,
the colour swirl of a precious stone.
Even though it's an aberration, almost May-like
in the middle of February.
I'm out for a walk:
to close the greenhouse doors
that I vented during the day,
with the news of an arctic wind
snow serpent
slipping in from the north tonight.

Usually on these walks
I try to invent lines of poetry,
something about the low clouds and how they roll over
on their backs like bear cubs,
paw at the ones above them as they wisp past.
Walking at a brisk pace,
almost speed-walking, taking in chunks of air,
another line comes to me by another poet:
Robert Lowell quotes Robert Frost
in a sonnet, where he talks about his two adult children
having gone insane, "How little my good health
ever did anyone near me."

And that always makes me think of Jake and Maya.
How does this vigorous walk help them?
All my Tai Chi, yoga, and Japanese sword practice,
all that blood through the veins
around muscles, rivers around mountains?
how does that help Jake with his Muscular Dystrophy?
How does it comfort Maya's feeling
of being left out all the time?

I remember when Jake was born
the baby next to him had a cleft lip,
which pierced me, the look
on his parents' face. Everyone else
counting fingers and toes, beaming.
And my little guy – his one visible blemish
was a crooked toe on his left foot
next to the pinkie toe,
and me thinking at the time
how someone was going to love
and kiss this one defect of his
when he was older. I silently named him
Jakey of the Crooky Toe.

How little I knew then.
And what do I know now? I close
the last house, mud thick on my boots,
just as the first flakes whip in.
I drink in deep draughts of winter cold
and raise this glass of sky
in health to us all.

Last thoughts

Five birds on the very top
of a bare tree head.
The birds are black.
They're like the last thoughts
before we die.

Like the lost notes that didn't work
in a Beethoven piano sonata,
or the leftover punctuation
after someone pulls apart a novel
and puts it back together.
The extra parts.

They look like late clinging leaves
that need a good wind
to shake off the glue.
But still I can make out their birdness?
the quiet sitting, the wing lift
to peck under.

And they will fly off.
Not one by one, but all together,
at the sound of the propane bird blasters,
used to scare them away
from the last ice wine grapes.
Fly together at the sound
of death walking into my house
as he slams the door behind him.

The Light Load

I used to carry him as an infant
wrapped in blankets
between the bare pear trees,
between the branches
like old fingers ready to snatch us
out of the moonlight,
sky and night forged
into a sharp January blade
that cut through our coats.

The grape wires sang
every meadow bird's song,
whispering like
the sound of stars stretching apart.

I'd walk all the way
to the neighbouring raspberry canes,
slow-chant to him
until he fell asleep. I could feel his weight
drop as though staying awake
required lifting the sky up
for everyone to pass under.

Through the days, months, years
he grows thicker with each sleep.
This simple vow:
You will never be too heavy for me to carry.
Asleep in my arms,
I take him up the creaking stairs
of an old man's back,
and lay him down into
the soft cup of night's fingers.

NOTES

All references in the poems to paleoanthropology and archaeology were taken from Ian Tattersall's excellent book on human evolution, *Becoming Human: Evolution and Human Uniqueness* (Harcourt Brace & Company, 1998).

Muscular Dystrophy: At the age of 5 Jake was diagnosed with Duchenne Muscular Dystrophy. It is generally described as one of the most common and most devastating human genetic diseases. Affecting 1 in 3,500 live-born males, it is an X-linked recessive disorder which strikes all world populations equally. No therapies exist which are capable of slowing the lethal progression of the disease: boys first show overt weakness in early school years, show a steady loss of muscle tissue, are wheel-chair-bound by age 14, and succumb to respiratory failure by age 20 unless ventilated.

The Art of the Japanese Sword: *Iaido* is the traditional, classical study of Japanese swordsmanship. The physical practice involves drawing, parrying, cutting, and various methods of returning the sword to the scabbard. The practised forms are known as *kata:* prearranged scenarios where the student repeatedly practices different angles and approaches to an oncoming imaginary opponent. This practice is studied more as an art form now than as an actual fighting method, emphasising correct form and efficiency, raising of the spirit and sharpening the mind. Nicklaus Suino (*The Art of Japanese Swordsmanship*), and Gord Warner and Donn Draeger, (*Japanese Swordsmanship*) are the definitive authors on this subject.

The Orchestra that Would be a Train: based on an orchestral recital of Bach's *Concerto for Orchestra* that I took part in, years ago in a Montreal synagogue, and described by members of the amazed audience as the first time in their recollection that Bach ever sounded like Schoenberg.